Ten Things You Need To

Nigel Morris-Cotterill

Nigel Morris-Cotterill

Ten Things You Need to Know about Dealing with Death

Nigel Morris-Cotterill

Legal Stuff

Ten Things You Need To Know About dealing with Death

ISBN-13: 978-1507730126
ISBN-10: 1507730128

Contact: Nigel Morris-Cotterill : via www.countermoneylaundering.com

All trademarks are acknowledged.

V1.0   20150126

Dedication

For Elizabeth Mary Cotterill
née Gibbs
Loving and much loved wife to Roy
and mother to John and Nigel
Grandmother to James and Ben
Daughter of Gladys (née Morris) and Arthur
Mother-in-law and friend to Mimi, Jacqui, Nejet and Jo.

1929 - 2015

And for Roy and John
who carry the burdens
while I am far away.

Introduction

For a long time, I was a solicitor in general practice and although my specialism was complex litigation, over the years I had a lot of experience in dealing with the elderly in a wide variety of physical and mental conditions and the bereaved of all ages.

When my own mother died, I realised that so much of what I had learned, of the experiences I had seen and the help I had been able to give remained with me and I was able to stand back and see myself and those around me with the eyes I'd been privileged to develop as a result.

I gave basic rules to my father. He laughed and thought that it was amusing to have a structure that he could refer to when he found circumstances became difficult.

The fact is that, especially for the first really close death, most of us have no idea what is happening. Yes, we can do the administrative tasks and we can robotically clean the house and feed ourselves but we don't really understand why we, emotionally and logically, respond the way we do. Worse, we are scared by our lack of ability to understand and control those responses. This book isn't about why we feel like we do: it's about how we respond and some very simple coping mechanisms.

We worry about the wrong things and we feel all kinds of illogical emotions and, because we don't understand those, we worry even more. We try to come to terms with the big picture when, at such times, all we can understand and deal with are small details.

We are terrified that our memories will fade or that we will remember the "wrong" things, or that we will somehow fail to show sufficient respect or, even, to mourn in a socially acceptable way.

Here(expanded, embellished and with a bit more humour) are the ten rules that I told my Father.

He doesn't laugh at the rules now.

Death is shit. Being the one who is left behind is even worse. You can't get a grip on basic things, you burst into tears when you don't expect it, you laugh when you don't expect it, you get angry with people who don't deserve it, you get frustrated because you have no control and you get frightened because it's not only the familiar horizon that's changed, it's also the ground you need to step on next. It seems as if nothing is or ever will be the same again and in one important respect, that's true. But the world around you goes on doing what the world around you does. There will be small changes, perhaps in the way people treat you, for a while but then, while people won't forget quickly, the world will carry on pretty much as it did before. The same people will smile as did before; so will those who scowled. While your personal world has ruptured, for everyone else, it's not significantly different and, in sometimes that's hard to deal with.

The ten rules here won't stop you grieving. Quite the opposite, in fact. It's important that you grieve as you think is right for you. Mostly, these rules remind you of the common sense that you lose during times of grief. There's nothing clever, nothing world shattering, just some brutal realities because it's important that there is a voice of pragmatism. There are no mealy mouthed words, no ambiguous expressions, no social-worker or soft-psychology tones. It's plain speaking for a time when you have enough to deal with without having to translate or read between the lines.

When someone dies, there must be a focus on the living while respecting the dead. It's not a balance: it's an imbalance in favour of the living. But emotion and convention push that balance the wrong way. This book adds weight to the side of the scale you are standing on, to help you remember that you are the most important person in this situation.

Thanks, Mother: without you, I would never have thought of writing down these rules. And Father: keep reading them so you don't forget them. That's why they've been written down.

For everyone else: I hope they help.

Nigel Morris-Cotterill
Kuala Lumpur, 2015

The Ten Rules

1. If you didn't make it happen, it's not your fault.

Ten Things You Need To Know About Dealing With Death

Normal, rational people become irrational in grief. They ask themselves over and over again if there was anything they could have done to prevent the death.

The answer is almost always "no."

If you didn't call an ambulance straight away while you tried to assess the situation, then you did nothing wrong.

If you didn't hide or throw away essential drugs, or administer the wrong drugs or the wrong dose on purpose, you did nothing wrong.

If you didn't throw a plugged-in hair-dryer into the bath with the person or push them down the stairs on purpose, you did nothing wrong.

If you spent some time paying attention to your own life instead of visiting all the time, if you didn't pick up every phone call every time, if you didn't speak to that person every day, you did nothing wrong.

If you didn't spend every minute of every day by an ill person's bedside, you did nothing wrong.

Are you getting the picture? The only way you are to blame is if you were obviously neglectful or if you did something that actively caused or speeded along the death.

And there are very few examples of where that happens.

2. You are the most important person, now

Ten Things You Need To Know About Dealing With Death

Death is surrounded by all manner of rituals and ceremonies. They are based in ancient ideas of lighting the way from earth to heaven. They are a way for the living to say goodbye to the deceased and they have value. They are also a way for friends and family to show support for the bereaved. Think of a funeral as an old fashioned version of a social media page where everyone sends messages of support and tells stories of memories but they do it face to face (remember when we used to do things face to face? It's nice).

Having said that, it's absolutely vital that the focus is not on the deceased but on those who are left behind. Being the one who is left behind is hard. And it's hard for all kinds of reasons you don't expect.

You are the most important person, now.

It might sound ridiculous but many couples have clear demarcation lines in their roles and when one dies the other doesn't know, for example, where the spare towels are kept; or the survivor will follow a normal habit of enjoying a joke with someone who, halfway through, he realises isn't there.

These are the devastating moments, the moments when the survivor realises he is suddenly responsible for everything and that he has no one to turn to for little things. It's when he realises that everything that was normal will never be normal again. The recognition that from now he has to build a new normal.

After the first rush of messages and visitors, the isolation and loneliness and fear sets in as friends and family gradually reduce contact levels. Of course they do: they have their own lives to lead.

So your primary job, as the survivor, is to prepare yourself for this.

First, recognise that things are as they are, not as you want them to be. A big part of your world has gone but the rest of your world is as it was. No matter how many times you shout out "where are the damned towels?" they are not going to move to a place you want them to be. Nor, incidentally, will they shout back "we are here." The coffee and sugar are in the same place as usual and the milk is, as usual, running out.

If your household routine was that your loved one took something from the freezer for lunch, then you need to put that task into your routine. Try doing it when you make your first coffee of the morning. It will make you upset, "she used to do this" would be a normal reaction. It's OK to react like that and it's OK to be upset.

It's not easy to prepare for life without a loved one but there is one extremely valuable thing you can do straight away. You need to make sure that you begin, as soon as possible, to have a routine that makes you do all the things you need to do in a day, a week, a month. Set up a check list that includes changing the bed-sheets, cleaning the toilets, doing the washing, doing the ironing, checking the larder...

Number one on that list? Get yourself out of bed, have a proper wash, scrub your teeth until they gleam and your hair until it shines. Wear clean clothes. DO NOT let your standards drop because there is no one there to see. If your loved one would have told you to tidy yourself up, then do it. Being sad is not an excuse for being a slob.

Remember the old expression "clothes maketh man?" Well, it's got a lot of truth. If you dress without sufficient attention to yourself, you won't pay enough attention to yourself in other areas of your life. And right now, paying attention to yourself is the most important thing you can do. You have to monitor yourself and your own state of mind and your living conditions. No one else will do it until you have fallen so far that people turn their noses up at the smell or laugh at your awful clothes. So head that off now by making sure you keep up the standards you've always had.

If you can get to the shops, go at least once each week. Support local greengrocers, butchers, fishmongers, small owner-managed supermarkets. They will start to recognise you and will give you a cheery "hello" that you won't get in supermarkets. If you are fit enough, go to the outdoor market. Your senses will be assailed by the noises and the smells and the hustle and bustle. For a while, you will have to concentrate on something other than your own sadness. That's a good thing.

Beware: you will soon be surprised by how fast your brain recovers. Think of the way your brain works as if it's two balloons in a bag. There's only so much space in the bag but the balloons are fighting to take a bigger share of that space. Your brain is a battleground in which the emotional part of your response to death takes an early advantage and pushes the logical part of your response out of the way. At that time, you think that the emotional response is all that is happening but, underneath it, the logical part of your brain is preparing its own response. It lets the emotional part run around, starting to wear itself out and then the logical part starts to re-establish itself gradually nibbling away at the emotional part, starting with the least strong emotions. Over time, they gradually come into balance.

That time can be short or it can be long but one thing is sure: when your emotions are raw, you think it will take a long time but it happens much faster than you expect.

When it does, you will find that you can concentrate much better, in some cases you will develop a focus on the task in hand that you forget all manner of things around you. During the stage of greatest emotion, you will want to sleep a lot. As the logical stage begins, your need for sleep will diminish. Ironically, you will sleep better as your emotions slow down and so you will feel more rested, with less sleep. That, of itself, helps the logical part to re-establish itself.

The only thing that spoils this system is if you suppress the emotional part right at the beginning: if you do that, then the emotional part still grows but it becomes harder to overcome later, as if the balloon is denser rather than squishy. It can take a very long time to start the grieving process fully if you delay it, even by a couple of weeks.

So don't be embarrassed to start grieving straight away and don't let anyone rush you.

If you want to take a day or two to do nothing or think, then take it.

Ten Things You Need To Know About Dealing With Death

Ignore anyone who tells you that certain things must be done in a certain way or by a certain time. There are almost no strict rules for a timetable for dealing with the legalities surrounding a death. Sometimes religious groups want various rituals and timetables: that's fine. Tell them to arrange them and that you are too busy being upset. It's your grief, not theirs. Don't let them take control of your time. Turn off your phone, unplug the doorbell. Go to a hotel and don't tell anyone. If you want time alone, take it and stuff them.

They are not important .. you are.

Also, people will tell you that it's important to talk about it and they are right. But there is a condition: it's important to talk about it when you want to and with the people you want to talk to.

It is not helpful to be confronted with a raft of people, all with the best of intentions, who think you should talk to them. Right then. Or to make an appointment. It's stupid: they are trying to impose a timetable on you, to tell you how you will feel at a particular date and time, even how you should feel right now.

If you want to talk about your loss to that person then say so, if you don't want to talk right now, say so. Say you will ask if they are free when you want to talk about it. Do not make appointments and tell that person you do not want to make an appointment. This is especially so if it's a professional: why should your grief fit in with their diary?

17

If you want to talk to that person about the weather, sport, politics .. in fact anything that does not directly relate to your loss, then tell them so.

Set boundaries.

If you want a "normal" conversation, then make it clear that that is what you want. That is every bit as much a part of a successful grieving process as going over the same sad stories with visitor after visitor, professional or otherwise.

Don't always try to be strong. Look: we English love our stiff upper lip, we do our laughing in public and our crying in private. We, as a nationality, don't like public displays of emotion. And for sure, we are uncomfortable if we see someone in tears in the supermarket, for example.

But it's a fallacy that we must bottle up our emotions until we are entirely alone. It's OK to have a little weep, even if friends or family are there. It's OK to decide to sit on a park bench and have a cry. Sometimes someone will ask why and you can tell them. Don't give a full history, don't go into detail. Just tell them the single most important point: the person who was half of your life has died and you miss him/her. Thank anyone who has asked for their interest and say you will be fine in a couple of minutes. And you know what? You will be, because you won't feel so alone because of the kindness of a stranger.

And it's OK to cry in front of friends and relatives. You don't need to talk: they know and understand your upset.

Ten Things You Need To Know About Dealing With Death

3. Don't feel bad about feeling bad.

Ten Things You Need To Know About Dealing With Death

You will have seemingly non-stop sad thoughts. That's fine. Don't worry about it. Feeling sad is good: it means you are doing two things - remembering someone close to you and thinking about the future. Sometimes thinking about the future makes you scared. That's fine, too.

The old Chinese proverb, a journey of a thousand li starts with a single step, is exactly what you are experiencing. Worse, no matter what some people will tell you while you might know where you need to get to (even though a part of you doesn't want to get there) you have no map. There is no GPS for navigating grief. It's a horrible, complex and ultimately unmapped area of life.

Death is scary: it reminds us of or own mortality. Life's a ticking clock, every heartbeat working steadily, inexorably, until it stops. When we see that in others, it reminds us that it's going to happen to us. We don't like it. We hide it, we use all kinds of words that death isn't permanent (and some people, of course, believe that it's not and that's OK, too).

Say "died" not "passed" or some other pseudonym: it will help you face the realities.

What's the number one cause of collapsing into tears? I don't know but I suspect that it's "She used to do that." Everything from putting away the milk you have left out to putting cream on a scar that, now, you have to ask someone else to do, from laughing at some silly random thing to a word or a phrase in response to something. There will be a million tiny things that remind you. That's OK. It's good. It's nice. It's honouring a memory and a love that continues. These are very good things. You should not worry that you feel them. You should be more worried if you don't.

But don't wallow.

Do stuff: don't put off dealing with the myriad people, companies and departments that need to be told about the death. You will force yourself not to pretend it's not happened.

Most importantly, don't think there is something wrong with you because you feel sad. There isn't. You already feel bad - to compound that by feeling bad because you feel bad is the first step on a spiral to depression.

Don't worry about others around you. After you lose a loved one you, and only you, are the most important person. It's like being on an aeroplane when the aircrew tell you to put your own oxygen mask on first, before helping those for whom you are responsible. At first, it sounds heartless but then you realise that if you don't look after yourself first, you will not be able to look after them at all.

Don't expect to be on top of everything. You will be absent-minded. You will put the milk on the doorstep and the cat in the fridge.

OK, so you probably won't do something that ridiculous but you will do some things that make you ask if you are losing your marbles. Don't worry: you are not.

You will lose things because you put them down without making a mental note where you put them. Why? Because we prioritise and at the moment you put those things down the priority was a) your mind was on your grief b) you put them down because you didn't need them at that moment and c) you put them somewhere safe so they didn't fall on the floor. What was not on your list of priorities was "I'll put them here so I can find them easily later." In fact, you barely noticed where you put them.

Another system, then. Every morning, walk around with fresh eyes and see what is out of position. Pick those things up and put them where you expect them to be.

See how your day is taking shape?

Personal hygiene and dressing
Boil the kettle for coffee and while it's heating, choose something for lunch
Make the coffee and put sugar in it, even if you don't usually take sugar in coffee.
While it's cooling collect the things in random places and put them where they belong
Take the coffee to your favourite chair and sit and enjoy it, watching the world go by.

Try it: in the first half-hour or so of your day, you have established a routine that shapes your entire day and sets it on track and you are already four pleasures in:

being clean and tidy
smelling the coffee
choosing some food to look forward to

relaxing with a hot drink with some sugar to give you a boost.

And while you do that, just think how many of those people dashing past your front window have been able to have so many nice things so early in their day. Not many, because they are always in a rush. But you, taking your time, doing things in order, have miraculously started your day in a much nicer way than them.

Little pleasures make a big difference.

Find your own routine if this one doesn't work for you.

Or embellish it: how nice would it be if the first thing you did, even before filling the kettle, was to put a croissant into the oven for five minutes and to have that, with butter and jam, with your coffee?

Don't make crumbs!

All of these things help lift your spirits a little bit.

And when the gloomy thoughts come, you know that they are the transient thoughts. You know that you can send them away, that feeling sad is, to a degree, a choice not a curse. And because you know you have a tiny, tiny degree of control, you know you don't have to worry that being so sad is a permanent state of affairs.

In short, you don't feel sad because you are sad, you don't feel bad because you feel bad. You feel sad and bad because of your loss, not because of your resistance to it. It's that derivative "Why am I so sad, why can't I get over this?" that is so corrosive. Being sad is a good thing: being worried about being sad is a very bad thing.

Ten Things You Need To Know About Dealing With Death

4. Not everything that is sad is bad.

Ten Things You Need To Know About Dealing With Death

I should credit this Rule to my brother: he said this when my best friend's mother died. There are times when the balance of life has tilted the wrong way and being dead is better than being alive. When that happens, we should be sad for our loss but glad for the person.

Some faiths talk about "going on to a better place," and that thought helps many people come to terms with the loss of someone for whom that balance had gone too far.

Some adopt a different stance, saying that life is short and death is for ever. They take the approach that sooner is better than later for someone who is suffering.

What matters most is not what you believe but that you do believe, and that you believe that a person's life as we know it has reached its end.

Obviously, sudden unexpected deaths due to unexpected circumstances e.g. an accident or violent crime don't fit this pattern and it's more difficult to come to terms with that in this way.

However, the vast majority of lives do not end unexpectedly: as the old medical joke goes (a joke that some politically correct fool criticised a medic for, causing him to be disciplined), sometimes the right thing to put on an expired patient's notes is "JPFROG."

It stands for "just plain fucking ran out of gas."

It's sad but it's not a bad thing.

And black humour is a defence mechanism: so don't feel bad if you want to make bad jokes about a good person. It's normal and it's human. It doesn't mean you are a bad person. If it helps you, then it's good.

Nigel Morris-Cotterill

You don't have to be sad all the time.

In fact, you shouldn't be sad all the time.

It's important that you know that, often, death is the least worst option. And sometimes, it's the best option.

Chronic or a series of acute illnesses over a period of time destroy the quality of life and, ultimately, take over the personality of the victim. It might sound strange to talk of someone as a victim of life but that's what they are.

Life gets us all in the end.

And for many, although they are scared of dying, they are not afraid of being dead. For them, while being well would be best, being dead is a release from a miserable, painful and hopeless existence.

This is not a plea for euthanasia. It is not a suggestion that a third party should decide that someone's quality of life has deteriorated so far they should not be looked after. It's a recognition that some people don't want to spend the last years of their lives hooked up to machines that breathe for them and are fed through a tube; some people don't want a life where they cannot move unaided and therefore spend their lives in bed being increasingly weak and uncomfortable; some people don't want to spend their lives in a drugged up, vague, state because, without drugs, they are in unbearable pain.

Some of those people reach a threshold of tolerance and decide enough is enough and quietly drift away.

We should not despair for them now: their torment, which in some cases lasts years and years, is over.

Ten Things You Need To Know About Dealing With Death

We should be happy for them that whatever they believe happens next will be better than that which has been happening lately.

That's hard, because we transfer our own hopes, wishes and fears onto that person. We should avoid trying to do that for that way madness lies.

We've enough to worry about without feeling that a person who drifted away quietly and peacefully didn't, at that point, want to go.

5. There is no timetable.

Ten Things You Need To Know About Dealing With Death

Grieving takes as long as it takes.

Some idiots will say "it's been three months. Get over it." If that's their attitude then good luck to them when someone close to them dies. If they care enough about someone when he's alive, then they'll care about him when he's dead.

Don't pay any attention to anyone who says you should follow a timetable, that stage one takes x weeks, stage two y weeks and so on.

There are comments from stupid people in relation to relationships that have been repeated across the lightweight magazine sector saying that it takes half as long to get over a relationship as the relationship lasted.

They say that it takes eighteen months to get over a three year relationship. This is the same kind of cretinous publication that carries articles by women in their mid twenties who claim to have had, say, three "long term relationships."

When you've been married for fifty or sixty years, that's a long term relationship. Even by the contorted reasoning of the magazine writers, it's going to take the rest of your life to "get over it."

So let's be very clear: if you had a good, strong, close relationship you are unlikely ever to "get over it."

You will get over the grief: the hurt will dull like a knife left out in the rain. But it is probable that you will not, ever, forget someone you have spent all those years with, or even relegate them to "not very important."

So don't worry that, in five, ten, twenty years time you are still thinking about your loved one.

Don't imagine that there are set times for feeling this or that. There aren't. You didn't place a long-stop date on your love when you were together so why try now?

Death doesn't turn love off.

You will find other people that will meet most of the functions of your loved one. You must not think "I can't ask x to do that, because my wife used to do it."

Having people around you is not disrespectful; having help is not disrespectful. Even having feelings for someone else is not disrespectful.

The only thing that is disrespectful is to deny the love you felt for that one person who was at the centre of your life.

Do the administration as soon as you can. There are things that cannot be put off such as arranging a funeral, registering the death, informing official bodies and so on. But for the most part, people are in place to make those things quick, easy and as lacking in stress as possible. For sure, some have a self-interest and undertakers are sometimes (not always) prone to up-sell and at times of stress, it's often easier to go with the flow than to say no.

The reality is that, in life, most people I know would elect for the simplest possible coffin and avoid a very ostentatious funeral. It's family members that imagine that to comply with that would be seen as failing to mark love and respect that turn it into an event.

Ten Things You Need To Know About Dealing With Death

So if you know that your loved one would want simple, have simple: don't feel pressured into having a room full of flowers if you want a single rose on the coffin, and so on. It's your loss, it's your loved one's funeral. You should have what you want, not what is overtly or auto-suggested to you.

Some of the paperwork is hard: reading a will, even though you know what's in it, is horrible. It's like someone is slapping you in the face with a wet fish while jumping on your toes between slaps. There is nothing good about it. Every word is a reminder that the centre of your life has just been taken away.

If you can afford it, hand the whole job off to a solicitor. Good ones will do everything from transferring the electricity and other accounts to the survivor to paying the funeral account from the money that is collected into the estate. There will be some papers to sign but mostly, once the solicitor makes certified copies of the grant of probate, you will have almost nothing to do with the administration of the estate until it comes to distribution.

That, I have to say, is a very good thing. Some estates are complicated for no particular reason, they just are. Dealing with those complications is stressful and a constant bad reminder of your loss. So it's counter-productive for you to handle it. It's best to give the job away and focus on the good things. Keep busy .. but keep busy with good things not bad things. It's better to plant seeds and mow the lawn than to handle the administration of the estate.

Dealing with the estate is not a labour of love, it's a torment and a trial. Unless you have no choice, don't do it. It will prolong the negative parts of your grieving process.

There is, however, one almost fixed date. I've no idea why this is: it's the same when you leave home, when you give up smoking, break up in a relationship or a host of big changes, the worst time is three weeks after the event. It's the time when many resolutions fail, when you want to go home for a visit, when you take a cigarette when one is offered, when you call your ex. So many of those things have a correlation with bereavement that you should expect that three weeks after the death, you will feel extra-miserable. But so long as you are prepared, then at least you won't worry that you are having that bad time when you thought things were getting better.

Ten Things You Need To Know About Dealing With Death

6. The stages of grief don't happen in a tidy sequence.

Ten Things You Need To Know About Dealing With Death

There is common agreement: there are a number of stages of mourning and grief. These are

- denial (often accompanied by isolation) in which the bereaved do not fully accept what has happened. It's fine: if you want to feel that the person you loved is still next to you and can still hold a conversation with you then feel that. Don't let anyone tell you that there is something wrong with you because you still feel their presence.

But that has to be tempered with reality: while their spirit (or whatever you want to call it) may still be there, physically, they have gone.

- anger at whoever, whatever is to blame or where you can apportion blame. Often we will feel angry with the person who died. It's rarely going to be their fault. But in the process we go through, we want someone to blame and, as in life, in death we try to hurt those we are closest to.

We don't get angry with someone we don't know very well when he or she dies, we don't ask why they left us, we don't ask what we are supposed to do without them. We reserve those questions for the people we love.

But often, too, we will feel angry with doctors, nurses even entire hospitals saying they should have done more, that they didn't find a cure fast enough, that mistakes were made. The body is a complex machine: when things start to go wrong with it, there is often a cumulative effect. Treating one problem often causes another. The medics are upset when someone dies: mostly, they see it as a personal failure.

Nigel Morris-Cotterill

We have to recognise the reality: we wear out, parts of us break so badly they cannot be repaired. Sometimes, like a machine, parts of us simply get so old and tired they stop working for no obvious reason.

- guilt is where we move from saying someone else could have done more to prevent the death to thinking we, ourselves, could have done more. Mostly, that is simply not true. Mostly, especially to those close to us, we do as much as we can. In many cases we do more than we should and it compromises our own health and emotional well-being.

We feel guilty that we should have spent more time with the person, even though we had, in many cases, reached the limits of the time we could spend without severely compromising our own way of life. Yet we cannot be expected to devote our lives entirely to someone else: we have to make our own way. Our parents went out to work yet we feel guilty if we go to work instead of spending time with them.

- misery. It's OK to feel sad. It's normal to feel sad. It's OK and normal to feel alone, even unwanted. Mostly, that's not true but the feeling takes over from reality. The important thing is that you have to understand that what you feel is normal. Brutally, you are not a special case. You will feel despair, you will cry and often you will not know why. Don't worry: it's normal.

You miss those little things, the touch of fingers as you walk, the smile in the morning.. you suddenly realise what was so important about your relationship was the way you unthinkingly recognised each other in so many tiny ways. Some people find that having a pet helps: just so that there is another active being in the house, but one that's not always asking the world's most stupid question: "how do you feel?" When someone does, it's OK to say "Fucking miserable, how do you think I feel" then talk about the weather. See "Don't feel bad about feeling bad."

You don't have to be nice to everyone: it's OK to tell people you want to spend some time on your own and you'll call them when you need some company.

You are allowed to be cantankerous and grumpy: no one would expect you to be in a good mood if you'd just had a leg cut off so they shouldn't expect you to be any less moody when you've lost the love of your life.

- acceptance is the most difficult part: until this point, you've walked along a cliff, a couple of paces away from from the edge. You've not realised it but all the previous stages are a security blanket. But just as security blankets get smelly, old and worn out, so do denial, anger, guilt and misery. Moving to acceptance is frightening, like taking those last two steps to the edge of the cliff. It means accepting that your life has changed and will never be the same, it means leaping into the unknown. For sure, family and friends are a parachute but it's still you making the jump.

It's OK to be scared. It's OK to be hesitant. It's a big step and you have no idea how hard or soft the landing will be. But one thing is certain: people who tell you to "move on" are clueless and are not being helpful. Only you can make that decision, only you can know when it's time. Only you can know when you feel brave enough to say "I love you and I will always love you but I need to look after myself now."

It's important to realise that these steps are not a logical progression. They don't come in sequence, they don't fit a time line. They don't always come in this order and they don't come, get dealt with and finish.

They overlap, they rush in and rush out only to come back again like a bad cold. One minute you can feel sad, the next angry and the next sad again.

Don't worry. It's normal. There is nothing logical or tidy about dealing with the death of a loved one.

Ten Things You Need To Know About Dealing With Death

7. There is no time limit to grief.

Ten Things You Need To Know About Dealing With Death

Just as there is no timetable, there is no limit to the time it takes to grieve.

If you said you would love someone for ever and a day, then that's how long you will miss them when they are gone.

Death doesn't stop the clock on love.

Don't let people hurry you. It takes as long as it takes. Just as every love is different, so is every bereavement. Ignore self-help books and articles that try to tell you what is normal.

There is no normal.

Everyone is different and in this bereavement process there are two people, one living and one dead: difference squared.

Quite possibly, you will always - on some level - grieve. Don't worry. It's normal.

You will probably never "get over" the person and most likely never get over the relationship in the sense that you will push it so far back into your mind that you will almost imagine it was a dream.

But you must aim to get over grief as a primary feeling, as a ruling influence in your life.

Aim to remember, even to miss, your loved one but aim not to let that control your life.

Some people think that they can go to the funeral and say goodbye and that's a turning point. It is a landmark but it very rarely is marks a significant reduction in grief.

8. It's OK to think hard thoughts.

Ten Things You Need To Know About Dealing With Death

No one is perfect. Everyone can be a pain in the arse from time to time. Don't think there is anything wrong with you when you remember the bad as well as the good.

There is nothing wrong with remembering times when your loved one did something that upset you and made you angry and there's nothing wrong with being angry again now.

It's part of a normal relationship. You would remember it if she were still alive so don't worry that you remember it now she's dead. Your brain doesn't have a filter that says you must only think nice thoughts or that all bad memories are expunged when someone dies.

It doesn't work that way so don't worry that you are somehow tarnishing the memory of someone: you aren't - you are being truthful to yourself and her memory.

It's OK to say "sometimes she could be an absolute bitch," if it's true. You can remind yourself of things that caused you distress - and you should. Because now you are able to deal with them knowing that the circumstances that caused that stress have gone.

When people suffer chronic conditions, or a series of acute conditions, over time, the do change. And long term effects of drugs can also make the most mild-mannered person acerbic or worse. Now you can think the hard thoughts and you have the time and the capacity to forgive, knowing that when the problems were seemingly never-ending, perhaps even getting worse, that you didn't have the time or the emotional capacity to forgive, only to tolerate.

And no, before you ask, you should not feel guilty for not forgiving earlier. Remember you are human and can't be expected to be subjected to a difficult life just because someone else has become irascible.

Ten Things You Need To Know About Dealing With Death

9. It's OK to be relieved.

Ten Things You Need To Know About Dealing With Death

This page might have been called "don't feel bad about feeling good."

Watching someone decline, seeing them in constant pain is horrible. Knowing that the body is preventing that person doing what the mind wants to do is a miserable feeling: we feel sorry for that person, often a young agile mind trapped in an ageing body with restricted mobility. And when serious illness strikes, knowing that they will almost certainly need care and attention, is draining and a cause of significant worry. You will worry how you will cope with mood changes as they feel increasingly bad about their situation and the effect on others, you will worry about how you are going to care for them especially if they can't be left alone for more than a few minutes, you will worry how you will deal with helping them from place to place, from chair to wheelchair to bed. You will worry about how long you can do all of this and how you will pay for someone to help when it becomes impossible. You will do everything that's needed of you, often with little support, because it's what we do for those we love. We deal with it and we don't ask others for help.

And you do it with love and care and you don't often complain or moan, even when the jobs are distasteful.

But when it's over, when you don't have to be worried any more, when you don't see the pain on your loved one's face every time you look, when you don't see the slowly extinguishing hope that things will improve, your own quality of life suddenly improves dramatically. So many worries disappear literally overnight.

Nigel Morris-Cotterill

It is, in the simplest terms, a relief.

Being relieved is not a bad thing. It's a good thing. It means that you have done the best job that anyone could do in your particular circumstances. It means that your loved one knew she was loved until the end and that no matter what you stood by her.

She would not want you to worry now. She would want you to do the things you want to do, for yourself, to restart a hobby you've not been able to do, to go for walks, to spend several hours in the garden or tinkering with the car and not have to listen out for calls for help....

And you can do that. You will be able to concentrate on things because you don't have to listen out for someone else's needs.

One word of warning: just because you are not listening for someone else, don't forget to listen for the timer on the cooker and ruin your lunch because your pans boil dry! Maybe you should get an induction cooker so you can set the temperature and timer and it doesn't matter if you concentrate on something else and forget it.

It's safer anyway because there are no open flames to set fire to carelessly draped cloths, no rising heat to make pan handles so hot so the pans are dropped spilling boiling liquids onto you, no gas flame to blow out if you leave doors open and then, after you've closed them, fill the house with fumes.

Ten Things You Need To Know About Dealing With Death

10. Keep memories not reminders.

Ten Things You Need To Know About Dealing With Death

It's your house now. You can organise it how you want.

But remember: it's OK to be sentimental. Be sensible not ruthless as you build the house around your own preferences. But equally, don't let sentimentality rule the way you organise the house: do what you want, don't say "but that's the way she liked it." If you want it different, make it different. If there's no good reason to change, then don't change. And if you can't decide, then don't decide. There is no pressure on you to make changes right away or at all. If the status quo is comfortable, then don't change. And if you think you'd like something changed but you don't want to do it yet, then that's fine, too. Do things when you are ready.

But there are things that remind you of the not so good times, especially when recent times have been times of decline. So for your own well-being you need to deal with those.

Buy a bread-maker and use packet mixes to bake your own bread: nothing says "home" like the smell of fresh-baked bread and freshly brewed coffee in the morning. And it will make the house smell of something new. Put it in the centre of the house so the whole house smells good when you wake up, instead of hiding it in the kitchen and containing that wonderful aroma. Also, you get decent, fresh, bread into the bargain, instead of chemical-laden, processed, sliced bread in a plastic bag because that's what supermarkets will deliver. What a great all-round result!

Right now, in the early days, the house will smell like it's smelt in the recent past. Find ways to make it smell like it smelt in earlier, happier, times. Find the same furniture polish, use the same toilet cleaner, the old washing powder, even the old brand of coffee you used to drink. Smells are incredibly powerful and plug directly into your emotions.

If your loved one had a perfume you especially liked, put a light spray on the pillow. Hell, put it on a pillow and hug it while you sleep if you like. There is nothing wrong with memories, even memories that bring a tear to your eye.

Happy memories are best but bad memories are part of the package. The aim is to have more good than bad. And that's not as hard as it sounds.

But there are things that are detrimental to your attempts to overcome your loss. Those things are the constant reminders of the recent past, when the balance of life was tipping the wrong way. You want to remember the past before the decline.

Everyone collects things around themselves, some more than others. As mobility decreases, the desire to put things away only to have to go to fetch them next time they are needed diminishes. Independent people don't like asking others to fetch and carry: they would rather build a nest of stuff around them.

The trouble is that the nest becomes a form of security and they don't want to sort it out, what was a convenience for two or three things becomes a pile of things that "I might want that" stuff. Worse, often what is in the pile is forgotten so it builds up with duplicates.

The first job after a death is to remove those things that act as reminders at first sight. So, remove clothes from pegs and put them in the wardrobe. It's a brutal thing to say but they are not going to be worn again. You won't be ready to dispose of them but you don't need to see them every time you walk towards the front door. Clear piles of things from side-tables, window ledges, fireplaces, bedside tables, under chairs (do you have any idea how much stuff accumulates under chairs when no one is paying attention?) . Throw away obvious rubbish, safely dispose of redundant drugs. Put the rest, glasses, pens, notebooks in a box to look at later. Throw away circulars and catalogues for things that don't interest you.

DO NOT throw away anything that is even a little bit personal. You are not in a suitable condition to make that decision right after a death. Later, you will wish you had kept some things. You can refine your choices later. In a few weeks you will feel able to spend a day bagging up clothes for destruction or to send to a charity shop and get it over with in a single, miserable, day knowing that in general miserable days are relatively few. But now is not the time to throw or give away personal things because you will make poor decisions.

If you cook, then fine. If you don't cook, and the kitchen was your loved one's domain, then remove all the things you won't use from sight. Pack them away in boxes, Again, don't make rapid decisions. What usually happens is that someone who has rudimentary cooking skills but enjoyed great home-cooked meals will gradually learn to cook, sometimes even to bake. Lots of those those things in the boxes might come out again in a few months. Give away things you don't expect to use soon like bags of flour, baking goods and other things you don't like or don't know what to do with. Then sit down and watch some good quality cooking programmes. You will be amazed to see that some high quality food is extremely easy to make.

Use up all the food in the fridges, freezers and cupboards then start again. Think what you like - and if you want to eat food that your loved one was particularly fond of, even if you weren't, then that's OK. Many families are built around food and there is nothing at all wrong with reminding yourself of that, even if you are sitting eating a bowl of packet soup in front of the TV, so long as that doesn't turn into a major part of your diet.

In the immediate aftermath, some good quality ready-meals are a very valuable standby. But within a short time aim at moving away from them. They have too much salt, sugar and chemicals.

Don't live on tinned or other processed food. Eat fresh.

Eating fresh takes up part of your day as you prepare. It fills the house with happy smells as you cook. So long as you don't burn the toast or onions. Yuk.

Don't be afraid to have a glass of wine during the day or a slug of whisky in your evening tea. Do be afraid of having more than one. It's not a good time to start drinking!

Because you will be absent minded for a while, it's a good idea to check the house and see if there are safety improvements that can be easily made. Don't keep worn out or damaged equipment if you can afford replacements: sentimental is good but not where it compromises your quality of life. A washing machine that goes walkabout every time it spins is a nuisance and the fact that it was a joint purchase is not a good reason to keep it. But an ornamental vase, utterly useless if you don't like cut flowers, might be something you want to keep for exactly the same reason.

Nigel Morris-Cotterill

Good luck.

Thank you for reading this book.
These ten things helped my father.
Writing it helped me.
I hope it helps you.

For Roy

On the death of his beloved Mary.
January 2015.

May your heart be quickly mended
And your life be quickly healed
May your love shine ever brighter
And your world be soon at peace.

And if sometimes you feel
A hand upon your arm
Or hear a quiet whisper in your ear
Say "thanks for dropping in, dear."

You can hold that conversation
You can close your eyes in joy
Because your love goes on for ever
In ways Death cannot destroy.

-0-

Nigel Morris-Cotterill

60

CPSIA information can be obtained at www.ICGtesting.com
Printed in the USA
LVOW08s2033010216

473181LV00038B/1779/P

9 781507 730126